C000212491

Paws for Thought

Maureen Melvin

Illustrations by Geoff Crook

summersdale

PAWS FOR THOUGHT

First published by Chapmans in 1990
Also contains poems from *Paws Again*, first published by Chapmans in 1991

This edition published in 2007 by Summersdale Publishers Ltd.

Summersdale Publishers Ltd
46 West Street
Chichester
West Sussex
PO19 1RP
UK

www.summersdale.com

Printed and bound by Tien Wah Press, Singapore

ISBN: 1-84024-588-3
ISBN: 978-1-84024-588-2

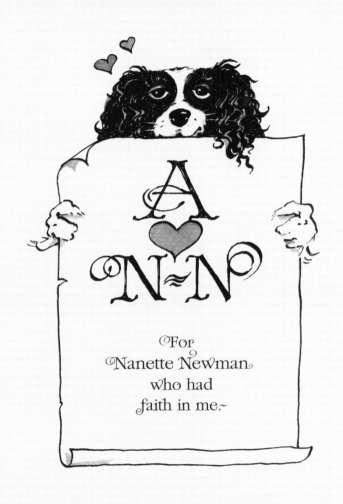

A ♥ N~N

For
Nanette Newman
who had
faith in me.~

Introduction

Abigail is a tricolour Cavalier King Charles spaniel aged six. She takes a great interest in current affairs and she is a keen television viewer, particularly of wildlife programmes. Since she was a tiny puppy she has shown considerable literary ability and has celebrated various occasions, including the birthdays of her family and friends, in verse. This is a small collection of her work, which she feels might be of interest to other dogs and their owners.

Author's Note

What do you know of a dog's life?
How much are you really aware
Of the intricate threads
That we weave in our heads
When you think we're asleep in the chair?

You know that we like to go hunting.
You know we are faithful and true.
But it may not be clear
That the dog you hold dear
Has a great deal in common with you.

You cannot have failed to observe us
As we pounce with a predatory paw
On the *Harpers & Queens*
And the smart magazines
That you carelessly fling to the floor.

We keep a keen eye on the City,
Observing our stocks and our shares.
We like cricket and ballet,
Museums and the Hallé,
And programmes on current affairs.

If you follow my life and adventures
You may be astonished to find
That your four-legged friend
Stands revealed at the end
With a soul and a heart and a mind.

A Life in the Day of Abigail

My day begins at 6 a.m.
Commotion at the door –
The Times, the *Mail* and *Sporting Life*
Come hurtling to the floor.

I grip *The Times* between my teeth
And take it back to bed.
It's great they're all asleep upstairs,
And I'm one jump ahead.

And when I've scanned the headlines
And absorbed the crossword clues,
I skim across the hatched and matched
And see who's blown a fuse.

She comes downstairs at last, and we
Enjoy a blissful hug –
Two minutes' gay abandon
Every morning on the rug.

She gets involved with orange juice,
With porridge, toast and tea,
And if I play my cards right
There's a Farley's rusk for me.

With breakfast done, I'm outward bound
To start my dawn patrol.
Besides which, there's a limit
To my muscular control.

I like to test the morning air,
Especially when it snows
And every frosted blade of grass
Is nectar to my nose.

Then back inside and up to bed,
My favourite grandstand view,
To watch her while she paints her face
And sprays her hair with glue.

If I detect a sign that we're
About to hit the store,
I round up all the shopping bags
And hover by the door.

You need your wits about you
When you're walking in the town.
Stiletto heels and pushchair wheels
Conspire to mow you down.

I'm glad to pass the time of day
With hound or Labrador,
But little breeds of lesser size
I usually ignore.

At last the shopping bags are full –
And not a jot too soon.
We have to get home quickly
For I always dine at noon.

The menu often varies,
But it's always gourmet fare:
Spaghetti, pilchard fishcakes
Or a sirloin, medium rare.

And when I've had my forty winks
And downed some H_2O,
It's boots and coats and walking sticks,
And up the lane we go.

I always choose the daily route –
She doesn't seem to mind.
Besides, if I don't get my way
I only lag behind.

I put the breeze up rabbits,
But their fears they soon forget.
They know I'm only playing
And I haven't caught one yet.

I tiptoe through the pheasantry –
A dangerous pastime this.
The farmer has a shotgun
And he doesn't often miss.

It's safer out beyond the wood,
Across the open ground,
And I can run for miles and miles
With no one else around.

If we should meet the local hunt
I hide behind a tree.
I know they're looking for the fox,
I'm glad it isn't me.

The fox and I are faithful friends –
I have his home address.
I wouldn't leak it to the hounds
However hard they press.

My working day begins at four,
I'm not a parasite.
I sharpen all my pencils
And I settle down to write.

I only do an hour or two –
I find it very hard.
My spelling is disastrous
For a cultured canine bard.

And when I've reached my target,
If the hour is not too late,
I study *The Spectator*
Then I know I'm up to date.

I follow through the book reviews
And all the serious stuff.
By then my brain is reeling
And I know I've had enough.

It's time for relaxation
And I often have a snooze
Unless they're showing *Mastermind*,
The Meercats or the news.

It's lovely by the open fire,
The embers glowing red.
But all good things must have an end
And soon it's time for bed.

I do my late-night guard dog bit
With fearsome bark and growl,
Which petrifies the fieldmice
And infuriates the owl.

With half a rich tea biscuit
To sustain me through the night,
I settle on my beanbag,
And she switches off the light.

It must be quite apparent
That a dog needs lots of sleep,
Not just for chasing spectral cats
Or insubstantial sheep.

For we have 'clouds of glory' still
To trail around our heads.
And that is why we sleep so sound
And linger in our beds.

Some dogs win championships at Crufts,
Some never get to shine.
But every dog must have his day
And this, my friends, is mine.

What's in a Name?

My name is Abigail of Course.
I've always wondered why
I have no proper surname
Like McGregor, Hunt or Bligh.

I scrutinised my pedigree
To see what it would show.
There's Rosamund of Ottermouth
And Merry Matelot.

There's Gorgeous Girl of Eyeworth
(A lady of the night!),
And Applecourt Delinquent,
But not a Course in sight.

I tried my *Great World Atlas*
To locate my title source.
I found a place called Corsica –
The French pronounce it 'Corse'.

So maybe that's the answer.
Though I'm British through and through,
I'm very keen on Sole Bonne Femme
And Mummy likes it too.

And signing cards for Christmas,
Which I happily endorse,
She writes: 'With love from Him and Her
And Abigail of Course.'

Down in the Mouth

When Things Are Said about my breath
It is, of course, the kiss of death.
And just to make things harder yet
They whisk me off to see the vet.

I don't know why they take that tone.
At least my teeth are all my own.
I've never had a jacket crown
Like other dogs I've seen in town.

The vet and I are special chums.
I sit while he inspects my gums
And if I need a small repair
He straps me in the dentist's chair.

He tips me up from north to south
So he can see inside my mouth,
And with a powerful jet beneath
He cleans the tartar from my teeth.

I'm fairly good at sitting still
Until I hear that dreadful drill,
But if I kick and thrash about
A hypodermic puts me out.

And then I don't mind what they do
Until I wake up, good as new.
My gums are healthy, pink and bright
And all my teeth are shining white.

I rinse my mouth with pink champagne
And spit it smartly down the drain.
It's not a waste, it helps me find
The bits the dentist left behind.

Back on my feet, and down the High
I flash my teeth at passers-by,
And no one looks the other way.
I'm flavour of the month today!

Cats and Dogs

'It's raining cats and dogs,' they say.
I can't imagine why.
I've never noticed dogs and cats
Cascading from the sky.

Why don't they say, 'It's raining rats',
Or skunks, or ducks and drakes?
It could be raining crocodiles,
Or porcupines, or snakes.

I wish they'd follow my advice
And find a better phrase.
But man prefers the status quo
And hates to change his ways.

So when I'm dressed for action
In my Aquascutum togs,
'You can't go out today,' they'll say.
'It's raining cats and dogs.'

God bless you, Mouse

There is Something in the cupboard in the corner by the stairs
And it's not as small as butterflies and not as big as bears.
At night it grows adventurous and runs around the house,
And at last I know for certain that the Something is a mouse.

When I was dreaming by the fire of strange and distant lands,
He strolled across the open hearth and paused to warm his hands.
My eyes were standing out on stalks, I quite forgot to chase.
When I pulled myself together he had vanished into space.

And now he comes to visit when the family is in bed.
He curls up on my beanbag and amazing things are said.
He tells me tales of derring-do and breaking out of traps,
And relatives with wooden legs and other small mishaps.

I find that he's a fieldmouse and he leads an active life:
In summertime he lives outdoors and picnics with his wife.
He roams around the countryside engaged on mouse affairs,
But in winter it's the cupboard in the corner by the stairs.

I'm sad to say when people are confronted by a mouse
They often have the vapours or run screaming from the house.
I think they should remember this behaviour may offend.
I like my little fieldmouse and I'm proud to be his friend.

Christmas Dog

I'm not too keen on Christmas.
It's not the time for me,
With holly prickles under foot
And needles from the tree.

The house is pandemonium
And no one wants to play.
It doesn't matter where I go,
I'm always in the way.

I get a Christmas stocking,
Like the others in the house.
It's filled with chocolate buttons
And a tiny sugar mouse.

I think that Father Christmas
Ought to mind what he's about;
He stuffs them in so tightly
I can never get them out.

They dress me up in ribbons
And a silly paper hat.
They even call me 'Christmas Dog' –
I don't much care for that.

The Christmas message – 'Peace on earth,
Goodwill to all mankind' –
Is bully for the human race,
The dog gets left behind.

If I could make a Christmas wish
Beneath the mistletoe,
I'd like to be in Bethlehem
Two thousand years ago

To watch beside the baby's crib –
The ox, the ass and me.
Now that's the kind of Christmas
I should really like to see.

Ballerina

I wonder what I'd look like in a tutu.
I've practised my positions at the barre.
There'll be noses out of joint
When I pirouette on *pointe*
And they realise I'm an up-and-coming star.

I'll never be a prima ballerina,
But I'd like to be considered for the corps.
They could put me at the side
Till I get into my stride,
And I'll promise not to end up on the floor.

Swan Lake, of course, has always been my favourite,
And I'd love to have the chance of going on
In a modest little role,
Like a duckling or a mole,
Cos I guess I'm not cut out to be a swan.

The Spice of Life

I am well supplied with tins of beef and liver,
And they rustle up a lamb's heart when I wish,
But it's purely supposition
When those experts on nutrition
State that dogs like meat – and only cats like fish.

I once struck up a friendship with a moggie
Who would sell her soul for mince or sirloin steak.
And if anyone should doubt it
Let us make no bones about it,
I, myself, would kill for kippers, cod or hake.

But now the pet food boys have had a brainwave
And they've come up with a cracking good idea.
How I wish they'd done it sooner –
Tins of chicken laced with tuna –
And discriminating dogs will raise a cheer!

Royal Dogs

I've never met a corgi,
They're not as royal as me
Although they're always out in force
Where royalty choose to be.

They haven't got a charter
To raise them from the ranks.
They can't drop in to swimming pools,
To theatres, shops or banks.

I have it from the horse's mouth
They snap at ladies' feet,
And other things have come to light
I'd rather not repeat.

No doubt they're in the running
For an edict of their own.
I guess they think they've got it made
With one foot on the throne.

They'll have to pull their socks up
And mind their p's and q's.
You don't win royal appointments
By destroying people's shoes.

Perhaps they should remember
The title 'Royal' is mine.
King Charles bestowed it long ago
And I'm the first in line.

Featherweight

My hunting skills are all revealed
When chasing feathers in the field.
The birds obligingly divest
Themselves of plumage from the nest,
And all their cast-off debris flies
And drifts and floats before my eyes.
Then I can leap into the air
And snap up feathers everywhere.

One morning when the wind was high
A lady, who was riding by,
Pulled up to watch my expertise
With wayward feathers in the breeze.

Now, as a rule, I'm not aware
Of anyone who stops to stare.
This lady, though, the forward kind,
Called out to see if we would mind
Her coming in to ask my name.
I knew she'd interrupt my game,

But manners maketh dog, I feel,
And came obediently to heel.

She studied me from head to toe,
And we were most relieved to know
The reason for the third degree –
She'd had a little dog like me.

This Henrietta, we were told –
A sporting type, just nine years old –
Had been out rabbiting for hours
And must have overtaxed her powers.
She ate her dinner, drank her drink,
Then to the garden room to sink
Exhausted on the cold stone floor,
She gave a cry and breathed no more.
We voiced our sympathy, of course,
To both the lady and the horse,
Suggesting, as we reached the gate,
Perhaps the dog was overweight.
The lady eyed my well-filled fur.
'Not half,' she said 'as fat as *her*.'

And with this shattering display
She wheeled her horse and rode away.

We plodded home with solemn tread.
No smiles were smiled, no words were said.
Once safely back, I crept inside
And tried to find a place to hide.
I wedged myself behind a chair,
I didn't stick out anywhere.
When tea-time came she didn't call –
No chocolate bones for me at all.

And later, in a dismal heap
I sobbed my portly self to sleep.

Next morning I recovered fast,
Determined to forget the past
And keep my friends and critics quiet
By following a rigid diet.
I'd buy myself a set of weights,
Some boxing gloves and roller skates.
I'd exercise and swim and jog
And be a snake-hipped, slimline dog.

BBC Points of View

I don't suppose you get much mail
From little dogs like me.
I'm so upset, I had to write
And tell the BBC.

I waited all the week to see
Some coverage of the show –
The championship at Crufts, I mean,
In case you didn't know.

The only programme I could find
Was late on Sunday night
When royalist Cavalier King Charles
Like me are tucked up tight.

I stayed up late to see who won
But got no satisfaction.
They gave it to an Airedale
Of Italian extraction!

Please will you ask the powers that be
To give us all a break,
And show the championship for dogs
While dogs are still awake!

Hospitality

I had a friend to stay last week –
It wasn't a success –
A grand Old English sheepdog,
But, my goodness, what a mess!

You couldn't see her eyes for hair,
She didn't even look
When I pointed out the pictures
In my favourite poetry book.

I tried to make her welcome,
I could see that she was shy.
I told her tales of shaggy dogs
But all she did was cry.

She wouldn't touch her dinner
So I offered to help out,
But that idea went down like lead

Since I'm a trifle stout
I showed her round the garden
And I took her up the lane.
She found the usual offices
Then lumbered back again.

She commandeered my beanbag –
I don't think that was right.
She fell asleep and never stirred;
I counted sheep all night.

She went away next morning.
I didn't feel the loss.
This, clearly, is a one-dog house
And, clearly, I'm the boss!

Heartache

I fell in love with a Labrador
When I was only three.
He would often stroll by the garden gate
In the evenings after tea.

He always gave me a friendly nod
And passed the time of day,
But he never touched me nose to nose
Or asked me out to play.

I saved him crispy pieces of fish
And chocolate bones from tea,
But I understood what I felt for him
Was not what he felt for me.

SWOON

One day he came with a jaunty step
And a lady by his side.
She was truly a golden Labrador
And destined to be his bride.

My heart sank down to the tip of my tail
When I saw the way things were.
I gave him my finest chocolate bone
But he laid it in front of her.

I saw him rarely after that
And I think he moved away,
But I used to wait by the garden gate
When the sun went down each day.

I never fell in love again,
And nobody fell for me,
For I lost my heart to a Labrador
When I was only three.

Wielding the Willow

I like a game of cricket in the fields or by the sea,
And friends will come from far and wide to play the game with me.
I pick my team at random from whoever seems the best
I'm captain of the The Ladies and The Bounder runs the Rest.

The Bounder is a hound I met when he was past his prime,
But rumour has it he was quite a player in his time.
His dignity commands respect from all the junior pack;
His strategy is masterly when planning his attack.

Our regular recruits include two Collies from close by –
Young Laddie who's a sprinter and Old Spot who's not so spry –
Two Labradors from up the lane who often cause a rift.
They have the killer instinct but they give the game a lift.

Now Tink, who hails from Devon, is a Lurcher acrobat,
A dastardly spin bowler and a demon with the bat,
But when she makes a catch she goes on running at full power,
Then swims off round the headland and is gone for half an hour.

Two Dachsunds, Port and Starboard, sail from Guernsey every spring.
They practise at the nets for hours, convinced The Game's The Thing.
They're not much good as batsmen, being stunted in the joint,
But Port is great at deep square leg and Starboard's grand at point.

With Busby, Fred and Charlie Two, all Cairns of high degree,
There's every prospect of a scrap before we break for tea.
But Sapphire, who's a Cavalier and star of stage and screen,
Can always be relied upon to keep the party clean.

Though Oscar is an obstacle, we have to let him play –
A plucky little Yorkie, most appealing in his way.
But while his partner wields the bat he cannot hang about,
He hurtles blindly down the pitch and runs the fellow out.

We find the wickets hidden where we buried them before
And mark the pitch precisely on the firm and sandy shore.
I put The Bounder in to bat, he knows that I'm the boss;
I use my double-headed coin and always win the toss.

I call the shots all afternoon and change the teams halfway.
On sunny days we carry on until bad light stops play.
There tends to be a problem over adding up the score,
It saves a heap of trouble if we finish with a draw.

When stumps are drawn and buried and the sun's about to sink,
We linger in the sand dunes with a sandwich and a drink
Reflecting on the highlights and the finer points of play,
And plans are made to keep in touch and meet another day.

From this athletic spectacle it must be plain to see
It's not the sort of cricket to impress the MCC.
But dogs like us are not concerned with how the game is run.
As Oscar has been heard to say, 'It's just a bit of fun.'

But I have dreams of greatness when I'm sleeping in my bed,
And no one knows the centuries I've made inside my head.
I stroll to the pavilion, and the sporting world applauds
When I retrieve the Ashes for The Ladies up at Lords.

Something in the City

for my friend Nick

I know you're very witty
And you're 'something in the city',
Although no one ever tells me what you do.
So I thought you might be willing
To assist me with a shilling,
Then I'd come along and spend the day with you.

When you leave the subway station
At your usual destination
I'll be keeping close behind you in the crush.
And I hope you won't outstrip me
For there's quite a lot to trip me,
With my brolly and my briefcase and my brush.

It will all be most exciting –
I'll be adding up and writing,
And I'll master things I never knew before.
When it's clear that I'm not swanking,
Just a whizz at corporate banking,
Then your friends will want to shake me by the paw.
And at lunchtime we'll go walking

If you're not too busy talking,
And we'll call in at a sandwich bar or two.
But if business is too pressing
We'll stay in and keep them guessing
With a steak for me and strawberries for you.

As the afternoon advances
I'll consolidate my chances
In a bid for quick promotion to the board.
But the speedy circulation
Of my canine inspiration
Will ensure that all the profits will have soared.

When the day is nearly ended,
And our homeward way we've wended,
Then we'll grab a Chinese take-away for two.
And we'll sit in your pagoda
With a well-earned Scotch and soda,
And I'll be a merchant banker, just like you.

A Birthday Card For Daddy

I wanted to buy you this picture
As a present from Mummy and me.
But the Wallace Collection
Agreed on reflection
They couldn't take ninety-five p.

So we went to the shop that sells postcards
And we found you a copy instead.
And I'm happy to say
I was able to pay
Without putting myself in the red.

If you searched through the Louvre or Uffizi
You couldn't do better than that,
And I think you'll agree
It's the image of me
With my feather, my coat and my hat!

Lend Me Your Ear

I know that Daddy loves me –
Of that there is no doubt.
He slips me lots of special treats
When Mummy's not about.

This high regard is mutual;
I was very fond of him
Until the day he went berserk
And gave my ear a trim.

He seized the kitchen scissors
And, somehow, contrived to shear –
By accident and not design –
Three inches off my ear!

Of course, he was beside himself,
And I was quite distraught.
I'm ragged and lopsided
And I'm listing hard to port.

When Mummy saw the damage
She was really in a stew.
I won't reveal the details,
But the air turned rather blue.

She says it won't take long to grow,
I only hope she's right.
I look like Orphan Annie
And I feel a perfect fright.

Next day, when we went shopping
It was more than I could bear,
I caught a Yorkie smirking
And my friends all stopped to stare.

Things haven't been too rosy
With my finest feature docked:
Poor Daddy's on probation
And the scissor drawer is locked.

I've been too vain about my ears,
Too mighty and too high.
'Pride goes before a fall,' they say,
And now I realise why.

Pointed Glances

There's a tea towel Mummy dotes on in the kitchen,
With almost every dog that you could see.
There are Boxers and Alsatians,
Pomeranians and Dalmatians,
But there's not a single dog that looks like me.

I've aimed some pointed glances at that tea towel,
And I think she's got the message loud and clear,
For with colleagues such as these –
Poodle, Pug and Pekinese –
I'm amazed they've overlooked the Cavalier.

I'll not be too surprised if, come next Christmas,
There's a special parcel waiting on my shelf
With a tea towel which discloses
Abigail in various poses,
Then I won't mind drying dishes by myself!

Soul Searching

I'm going to be an angel
When my life on earth is done.
I'm going to fly around the sky
And shine on everyone.

I don't pay much attention
To that silly rigmarole
That dogs don't go to heaven
'Cos they haven't got a soul.

Well, Mummy thinks I've got one,
And she's very often right.
She always says, 'God bless you'
When she tucks me in at night.

I've made a few enquiries
And that theory's full of holes.
There's someone up in Kemble Wood
Who stocks immortal souls.

It's my old friend the badger.
He's as clever as can be.
He stores them all in boxes
In a fallen chestnut tree.

You can't just go and buy one,
You have to pass the test,
Like helping toads across the road
Or birds to build their nest.

You have to rescue waifs and strays,
(I've done my share of that)
And learn to nod politely
When confronted by the cat.

I think I'll keep it under wraps
So no one else will know.
I'll pack it in my travelling bag
And take it when I go.

The soul will be my passport
But I'll need a few more things:
I'll have to ask St Francis
For a halo and some wings.

And when I've mastered miracles,
And earned some free weekends,
I'll hover over Gloucestershire
And wave to all my friends.